D0867451

WE ARE ALL
GOOD IF THEY TRY
HARD ENOUGH

We Are All Good

Publishing Genius
Baltimore, 2010

If They Try Hard Enough

Mike Young

Publishing Genius
1818 E. Lafayette Ave
Baltimore, MD 21213
www.PublishingGenius.com

Cover design by Rachel B. Glaser and Mike Young
Cover art by Lyndsey Lesh
www.lyndseylesh.com
Book design by Adam Robinson

ISBN 13: 978-0-9820813-7-2
ISBN 10: 0-9820813-7-5

Copyright © Mike Young 2010

Contents

I

II

III

for if You do

When they sang of what they had thus named,
they still meant You.
Martin Buber

Let's Invite Permission

Here, put that down. Let me show you a
kind of holy something. You're allowed to
maul this whole gymnasium of instigators.
I mean you're allowed to be cute, like that,
or you're allowed to feel anything you want:
knives and sponges, carnival wristbands and
chicken grease. Here, put me down. I feel
uncomfortable, but avowedly so. That's the
Theory of Radical Alterity. It's the only
catch; see also the riders of the bus who
genuflect when they pass over a bridge in the
hail. Feelings are expensive greeting cards.
You buy them several times a year and wonder:
how does the hologram work? The tiny songs?
They're a lark but not a marvel really.
Funny people exist—you've felt them!—yet
they seem to have no hand in the punch
lines. You always feel stupid when people
praise your feelings, which is why we have
VMAT2, the self-transcendence gene (or God)
but also a clause that lets us feel like c'mon:
a giant wolf. Isn't he the scheme? Kindly and
doomed, like an old sitcom boss's face post-
laugh cue. Faces are big to feel with, close
especially, like a good sheet fort in action.
We're allowed to wear the Other's favorite shirt.
My lips have cinnamon bun stains and old blood,
and you feel to me somewhere between coffee and
lamination. Here, put the flashlight down. Wait,
I also want to feel the light avow itself.
Maybe we can deal in bulb spaces. Here,
let me spill this dust all over your hair.

Do You Pray in the Shower?

No, but I do pretend to give interviews.
Which is another kind of complex, right?

Anything you can do, I can make a doll.
Zee mirror is a kind of punch clock, too,

and then you go, "Then so—" "Exactly."
Wouldn't it be nice to serve a head less?

Can't a guy say uh oh, chocolate maltballs?
Ride an antelope into the breaker room
or even be of snow on almonds generally?

This is this's fault, and I won't call you
"okay" unless that's really your name.
I wanted to show you more, but you were

in it, so I couldn't. Lillian zydeco hill bait.
I want to be useful as secret mouthwash.

If you rest halves of ping pong balls over
your eyes and indulge a bout of radio static,

it's like no one can judge you for being
afraid of LSD. It's hard to admit, but not all
of us will dance on your birthday at 4:52.

Look, they come in your house and nothing
is missing after they leave and you want to
thank someone. That's natural. I can see you.

God, grant me a belief in mostly everything.
Please don't make me call you selfish again.

Is This a Sitcom or a Sycamore?

All the things that made you feel better
can again. Still can. On a couch? Sure.
Play tennis until the tall lights flood.
Someone is flossing with tinsel still.
I am killing a carpenter ant just to watch.
Cherimoyas and pinball. Cues of skin by
skin like balloons all over your hair.
Others will sleep right on through your
nostalgia: that's what it's there for. In fact,
unpathetic crying is the holy grail of behavior.
File down each of your knuckles and drown
the flakes in various cups and I will play
match: Cessna gas, nutmeg cider, trestle oil.
Coffee makes you want to live a little bit
forever. Maybe I want to be the person in your
dream that breaks the news. Or maybe the first
told: "Guess what, Mike, you're in mine now.
We all know how to swim. We have one big face."
What I do know is the trick of all things wonderful.
It's that you can't thank them. They'll make you.

You Can Know That Wait Means Stay

Right away there's thinking. Right away.
No matter how much I want my face to moon
with no contortion, leave all talk to voiceovers.
Hands take after purrs. Nicknames remind us
mostly of the fun inventing them. Every beach
fire is a kind of desperate flag. Cops pull over a
riding lawnmower, and the man won't turn it off.
We walk the dike that crosses I-91. Headlights
pan like reasons. We're keeping warm. Cars aren't
fireflies, which is not even how I feel. "Funny isn't
the same as being happy," I tell you. Duh. Neither is
that. A family of tiny arsonists live in burned out
delivery trucks behind your neck. They are your
bad pillow. Hands wobble. It's never been infinity
with me. Infinity is something I can fist bump.
It's more like when I chew the top off a lightbulb,
and there's no blob of light to hold. Carry. Get
close. Let me eat your eyelash like a mission.
If we plant it in a divot on my cheek, maybe I'll
grow your love of coats. The lay of your wrist
when you're tired. What plays in your head after
you gnaw my finger, look at me, teething the skin like
wrapping paper you want to save for next Christmas.
Sometimes I know that I don't know what's going to happen
next, but I know exactly who I'm going to be with when it
does. This feeling is called kiss me. This feeling is called hi.
But maybe you're not thinking of anything. I've thought
about that. We're on a hillside. Night grass. Grass face.
And the sky is clear enough to see exactly how you feel.

for Carolyn

Giggle or Stop It

I will, of course, be there for whatever.
But only if I'm so famous I can't be held
against myself. My sense of humor in
real life is like the street person who
convinced you to give him money after
he moonwalked explicitly into your heart,
I mean tripped on a pigeon, I mean off the
pier to float above the invisible seals of
thirty-nine obligations, where we steal those
yachts and stand on our decks in bathrobes
trying not to acknowledge the In-And-Out
neon or the other quite entirely, quietly,
like trying to erase the word *you* from all
promotional material. We never did see
Laundromat Jesus or those tinfoil shoes
that weather divine since they would be
lying anyway, which is another way to say
trying too hard. "Let's ride the BART to the
airport," you said. "Then what?" "Germany."
Bravery's a lot easier under your ushanka.
Push the option on me to stop the orbit I take
around the tiny dwarfs of preoccupation.
Which sounds like a big halve-the-tides-via-
eye-games, but it's really just a need for an
alternate light source. Really I just want to be
quiet for a little while inside your quiet too.

All of These Parties
Outside the Microwave

My friend, I went to your stupid mine,
carried in obligation's very hot mitten.

Everything was ticked as Gift, Scar, or Luck.
The new parasail made you look post-history,

as we do feel, or feel-ish, long enough to
fuck up. I did that eyebrows thing like good job.

Then we stood on the roof, years of stilt training
between us. We chewed Sudafeds and ham, chuckled at

by all: all that passes for beloved these days.
Why is cake in the shape of a rocket not

you? Someone wants to draw your face and I say
ransom. When my friend makes a good joke,

my other friends are in the shower distantly,
as the minutes before sunset wait to be

picked for the dodgeball of sentiment.
Half the time I feel like U.S.S. Bitchface,

and all the people line up to pet me. Other-
wise, I cut burritos with a pizza slicer and you

laugh and I think, "If that is your real laugh,
go to sleep. I want to steal it. Don't go."

Sunday Morning Prayer
to the God of Emo Wood Nymphs

I went to a party in the woods.
I dropped my phone. Who cares?
I didn't want to look for it.
I had friends who were like come on!
I was like phones are so 1743.
I don't know. I was so dehydrated!
I think I stepped on a butterfly nest.
I don't know how butterflies "organize."
I had this one friend who tugged my coat.
I guess she found the phone under a fish.
I guess she had to wrestle the fish.
I bet that the fish was coordinating.
I believe coordination is a big scam.
I think the fascists are probably tall.
I always wonder about the anarchy symbol.
I don't know if the A's little arms curl.
I mean at the end. So whatever. Maybe
I am stupid, but u have a square heart.

Spend Time at You

What's honest? Is a body honest?
If it closes at all, it's in the night.

I don't get to laugh when I say I'm afraid
of faces. I think you're—I don't know.

I want to be more like you but I want to be
happy more. Arms lie asleep on purpose.

You can't read the handwriting on your
face. Sometimes I just agree with you,

I just do. I want to sleep in a body
double with an option for realistic

need. I don't want to talk with
everyone. You should feel special?

I want to be the write-in candidate
of all your idle night drift, and win.

When people cry it's like Oh boy,
so why would I look at you like

well? What do you say? No,
I will never do that. I'm lying.

Motivational Naiveté

There's nothing wrong with being quietly astonished.
Feta baked right into the bread, the woman who steals
chalk with her thumb, cute girls in wheelchairs and
librarians at the disco. Barry? He's an emperor of
cheese and a Mickey D's apologist, which is great,
like my roommate bought these jeans off eBay
but they didn't fit her, so she gave them to me.
Little cares whether you do, but it's hard to shrug
authentically, the world moving in bengal tigers and
hyperthyroids, like one person will demand you shave
and someone else will break a shot glass in your sink.
But weather is the opposite of history. And/or
March is great for seeing people you met in a bar
fight and thinking: Wait, I sort of punched that guy,
they look nice, I wonder where they got that
sweater, isn't it too hot for sweaters, what terrific
wind, maybe I will say hello and we can reach in
to graffiti exclamation marks and emoticons over
our memories. Maybe this will be the day I finally like
metal music because it's so nice out and I can't
think of the reasons why it's so tricky to just like
everything. There must be some. I'll let you know.

   for Barry

Is There Light Where You Are?

"Bewilderment is the new New Sincerity" —Heather Christle

All the new bewilderment is about hay fever tablets.
In this it resembles the blind men running from the
elephant. In this it resembles nude appliance repair.
We're pulled aside and told we're loved, but listen:
the mustard gas has to go. If I keep feeling this way
I will have to use a lot of emoticons. I will have to
stop lying to my children about the history of blues.
No more oyster ice cream, illegal haircuts, arc welding.
Stricter regulations on confession distribution.
Stop with the codeine-in-the-milkshake "accidents."
All the old bewilderment was about jealousy between
umpires, twenty-seven facemasks dunked in blood,
piled in the sink. It seems like only yesterday
we hired these relationships, and now look at the
mics on us, even when we're not under emotion.
"I like that—is it new?" "No, we know someone who
already likes it." Now we're even sold our minutes.
We can talk on the phone in the handicap shower.
If I keep feeling this way, I will need a mitten
my whole body over. All the new bewilderment
mops in the blue hour and respects donuts,
dismantles the game into aesthetic experience.
We're rushed from the gym and told, "Lay here
and dream of time machines very hard." Okay.
We're given six unlabeled jars and told, "Pick
the new honey." That one. If I keep feeling this—
wearing, I mean, a pillowcase and a white belt—
we will drop the bones in the heart slot just to
buzz, buzz, even as we're not supposed to buzz.

I have invented a new kind of poetry that alludes
to Operation, which is also a new kind of feeling,
which was already our new kindness at work.
When the batteries run out, promise that you'll
melt me in my sleep and stir me up with blue acid.
Keep the lights on through all loss. Don't forget:
brilliant also means that none of us can see.

If I Crash My Love Goes With Me

Excuse me. You've parked in the towaway zone of
my confidence. Until I'm archaic I'm attachable.
To covert wars with your black underwear.
To a rain that makes duct tape out of May.
The Me as Lincoln logs with feelings: solder
resin. Think of my picture open in Photoshop.
When feelings are easy—but then I'm in a
bus on the Hudson Expressway with a peeled
roof. Choke on my granola bar. Shaving kit
spills down the aisle. Mexican priest with a
gash and moans. A man holds a bushel of his wet
hair, bloody, rolls it up in a Snickers wrapper
and leans out the wreck's window to smoke it.
"This is an induction of a crash!" I tell my
court reporters, my career in tastes, my how-
itzers of pantyhose and yellow dresses in the
night. Some of you I've given perfect games.
Or seared a wink in cinnamon, honey, cinnamon,
for a great supper on TV trays with sex too.
I don't want a song vendor beside my turnoff.
I don't want a ride to the hospital, thanks.
The guests I love have done my dishes for me.
If you want to know whether I'm in love with you,
put an olive in a bowl of Dr. Pepper, put a blue
berry in an even larger bowl of coffee. Sodium
floats, bonds ceaselessly, shudders up against
pilgrims on the beach and mixes with the salt
they've brought. This started with you inside
me, which is something I'd like in a tinkle box.
I called you up because I almost died almost
significantly, and isn't there anyone to vouch
for the pennies I've spilled under the pillow?

When I die, haul a mattress to the quarry, wet
sheets, then please make it up like I just rose.
If anyone can do this, it's you. Congratulations.

Advice is Dead Long Live Advice

Account, really: royalty counts.
Crown the orphan hockey goons, tea
peddlers, lie menders, good drivers.
Then freeze. Pay someone to stall your
quiet. Go dredge for enough light
to make home by. Someone buy shovels.
Don't weep for that bobsled of fire ants.
Old solutions sunk you in this free for all,
jibbery King Saul and all. I've got his nose.
Don't I look like the new king of naked town?
If you'd figured it all out, I wouldn't need
to name your needs and let you nap here.
Don't go nodozing on that bulldozer.
Buy the best walnuts, bloody fits of
reputation. Steal circumstance. Milk
the leaders of the survey for their
no shit moments. Everybody needs a
moment. I would give you mine, but
sweetie, they ain't done. I'm not useless.
This is just where we're at right now.

The Original Sleep Sound Generator

In Japan, many people dream of building a log home.
Jennie Dickinson dreams of Columbia County,
a sparsely populated region of wheat fields.
In order to wake up I know I must force out a sound.
There is so much more to life than a place to store
and explore your mixture between desire and revolt
against great views and horse racing. Someone—
with my crackers I guess—runs around the corner
and disappears. Joel's Journal is a software program
designed to help you learn to hear God's shotgun.
In a ballerina wheelchair, a tween girl can record
a message from her favorite rattling window that
might become the sound of a roulette game in
one person's commentary track. "You sound
excited David." "You bet I am Bill."

for Sasha

Off to the Derby
With a Clean Heart

Will that work for you? If not,
jitterbug and more premium grade
exploitation is due soon. Check the
coupons. They solve a lot. Such as:
what are we going to exploit tonight?
I coupled with my apology. We sold
matching track suits to buy each other
matching track suits! Oh you! Zoom!
We're off! My apology has a limp thanks
to Mega-Crucifix: Crucifix on Wheels.
Soon to be a major NASCAR sponsor.
But lo and behold—actually, no:
breach of privacy. Witnesses are failed
lovers. Anyway, I will report the details
of our race to your favorite exploitation
coconut. You open it. Ain't shit without
you! Oh wait: I feel a lucky w00t w00t
afoot. The coconut milk will immerse
your liver in that white lie of health.
Who talks all this shit about lies?
Lies are almost perfect vegetable milk
for when you are in a kind of secret
bad mood. Take a train to the derby.
Dance all sloppy in the club car. Now
we've come so far, no? I don't know
where your tap shoes went. Did you—
everywhere? Really? Well. Wow.

Them's the Breaks

You should invent a retarded hemp android
instead of playing bingo with your mother.
Age is not just the good ship New Excuses
but a way to like sad foods and clean
less teeth. Each day I want a little
said, a little different said, of and to
my face. O a lark the range of human salt.
O the luxury of handling a person's care.
O why did you turn the cold water on?
Oh. Sorry. I only wanted us all to awake
mid-stride, amid the crockery thieves and
early bedtimes, stews and old sweatpants.
My thing is with getting from now on. Yes,
I would like to skip anything that lives just
so bad advice can have a job. But— but—
The reason I never met you at the depot is
not clever. Please let go. I will pass out.
I like to build small promises and sew them
fast, but people keep slathering me with these
looks—shit, just tell me what to do, okay?

Now That I Own a Door

Leave you outside, you said,
with the spider on my doorbell.
Well, maybe him? Does he want to
join me and drag-race an armored car?
Fill my molars with melted honey bears?
Stay up until two playing the mandolin
with me, lift me—it has a nice ring.
Listen, kid: all of your friends are
burnt sod and none of them want to hear
the name June laughed from a tailgate
outside a stadium of grass like tall women
thinking about something else when
they lean into bus poles, when they
won't push the door before a sigh.
Your best bets are cable receipts
and neighborhood popsicle brats
in Hulk Hogan t-shirts, asking after
more kids. No, sorry. Just a crust
of sleet—but let me check the burners
twice, then the last gimp of my Crest.
I will find one yet to let back in.

for Bryan

It Takes a Lot to Win, It Takes a Lot to Cry

Here in the overcoat of my heart you're a burrowed parakeet.
My anxiety's the phantom gut lump kind. Sometimes you turn
hands and hands in a kind of sign language just outside the
frame, and this is the style of exchange I'd most like to learn.
How much curry versus coconut milk? Is everybody made of
history and aesthetics? What's the practical amount of
guilt to carry if you love the way a stranger touches her
lips at an oh-shit recall? Why is my arm not a lilac tree?
Are we human or are we dancer? Life is never over being
cute with me. All in a sudden I'm sure the whom of us
is pre-set: checkered skirts, gestures of private demand,
like how the boy rakes his temples to think harder
which means I'm thinking in terms of infinite level design,
like where each Non Player Character has this agenda
dreamed up by some minor programmer and advertised
on the box: The People You're Shooting Also Have
Schedules! Listen: the world arose from a system of
small boredoms. Hundreds of Gods on the payroll making
pet projects of oil spills, cliff swallows, a floating couch,
a ball of stardust said to hitchhike Arkansas backroads,
fish with whiskers and the taste of lemon. Of lemon?
Of yellow. Tell me that taste isn't deep in the code,
giggled in by some guy in charge of beta testing
photosynthesis and noticed only after the game
embarks on its viral release. Daniel, I stole that whole
idea from Douglas Adams and what you really need to
know in this endless commercial failure of an MMORPG
is that the original point of the game was the ocean,
and how to make that ocean lead to different things.
Each and every person then is just an Easter Egg,
defined by gamers as a feature you cheat to find,
as a bug that you are too in love with to report.

   for Dan

Concerns About Love

Because of its small size and durable nature,
love is a persistent environmental pollutant.

Love is commonly made from copolymer plastics,
aluminum foil, titanium dioxide, and iron oxides.

These materials are not readily biodegradable.
Being heavier than water, love sinks to the bottom

of waterways and contributes to toxic sludges.
Most love is used only briefly. At the end of

use it is showered off, entering waste water systems,
or swept up for disposal in a landfill. Love is never

recovered or recycled. Because of its small size, love is often
lost or spread by humans throughout their environment.

Small organisms are unable to deal with love, as it is
inedible. Larger creatures can ingest it involuntarily,

allowing it to enter the food chain. Because of love's metallic
nature, static electricity can cause love to stick to body parts

or habitats. Some of the oxides love is made with can be
reactive when combined with other waste streams, particularly

in water. Love has very sharp and hard edges which are uncommon
in nature and a problem for very small life. When the same material

as love occurs in industrial situations as swarf, it is considered a
hazardous contaminant for which extensive safety measures are required.

Let's Build the Last Song and Sneak Away While Everyone Is Listening

I

When you are near me, I am a confident paper boat
in a bathtub full of Kool-Aid, where I tilt in circles toward
the drain, which does not worry me, for I know that a wet
hand will reach up and carry me into the kitchen.
We will eat goat cheese and asparagus. We'll learn
into each other by way of hoping we have guessed
right, and then be taken by *yes* and the silence that
holds *yes* the way I hold the hair beneath your hair.
Things that scare me include car dealerships at night
and the fact that snow cannot live inside my mouth.
Boom. That's it. Once on Belchertown Rd. I saw a ten foot
soldier with a deer rifle and a torn jerkin walk out of
1789 and into the woods. He left because he knows
I will protect you! You don't need to keep a grill skewer
in the soap dish. The world is something I will gather for
you and brush off like I'm cleaning a dryer filter. Let's plant
apple festivals in the radio. Keep one suitcase full of bees.
Listen, I like you so much that I want to steal your jokes.
Though you are a hand and I am a boat, we smell like
dancing. We make a new health. Dancing invented
us. Dancing is just putting yourself on inside out.
When you are near me, I feel as if I have caught the
only bus of the day somewhere in New Mexico and
you are the spy plane above us and the gingerbread
factory that the driver won't stop talking about. Except
no, wait, that's you, sitting in the aisle with your boots off.
You bite my shoulder. You have a smoothie mustache.
It is because your name does so much to me that I call you
many things. You ask me why I'm not asleep yet. I forgot
how to get there. For some reason I just hold you and float.

II

Sometimes I will melt a single gingersnap in the microwave
to wave back at the first time I did that, by accident, causing this
nervous yeti feeling to shove all my other feelings out of line,
to pilot the rickety go-kart of my constitution into a hay stack
over and over again, laughing like he'd never heard of
himself before. If you want to eat my brain, please note:
it's mostly carbonation. Make your arms my arms and tease mirror
me, who can get to acting like he owns the place. Phase him out.
Wear your red spy coat and put your hand over my mouth.
When I'm with you it's like they made it weird in the marmalade.
What a new color scheme you've invited! You remind me of facts:
1) Tablecloths were originally intended as after meal face towels.
2) One color that does not occur in nature is "Cheetos orange."
3) The watermelon is actually a very clever fruit from the desert.
4) Pickles come to us by way of Viking fisherman Gillis Beukel,
name mispronounced by English villagers so grateful for his brine
that whenever they looked at the guy they were already fondly
replacing him with their fondness for him. See, there go all my
best stories. I'm naked now. You don't want to hear how good
you are. We both hate describing empathy as a bucket contest.
Grace you can see because grace is when you wear another person's
light. No one wants a lover who admires them, like they're done.
We want to wake the person we're next to and whisper, "I can't make
it stop. Help." You know what I mean. With your legs around my waist,
dark in the kitchen, redwoods, cilantro, and Otis Redding's live version
of tenderness, the right version, the one we quit ourselves to know.

III

Do they talk about leaves anywhere else?
Martin Buber rides a bike through the construction
zone, as red maples over against the freeway drift
into record. The only unexpected change is a stranger.
In bodying forth I disclose. You made me check the
deadbolt, you said, "I don't even know you." You passed
out in my polo. With my hand I led yours over your skin,
a crook in your spine. "Sometimes I imagine that I'm
my skeleton," you said. All real living is meeting.
All real light presents. We didn't like Koch's ode to
orgasms, which Buber explains by eating a tuna
sandwich and inviting us to watch. Danny Devito fakes
a nap in the back of a U-Haul and kicks you in the
temple, whispering, "The Zulu word for 'far away' is,
in our sentences, 'There where someone cries out
O mother, I am lost'." You're not asleep, you're on
line, confessing that you've tucked in your pet knife.
Feelings are stray flamingos that visit unsummoned
and wrap their necks around the now we're in.
Leonard Cohen salts my eggs with Percocet, stays
casual about his skepticism of my attitude toward
protein, but most importantly he lets his hair down.
Most importantly, he stays. We're pretty awesome,
okay, but we are still alive by coughing through
harmonicas. If there are thoughts inside of which
we shiver, there is Buber in a cape he's sewn of
Thou and lake sheen. He would agree to never wash
the Dick Tracy shirt. What he'd say is, "Don't take her

to Oregon, tell her Douglas fir and low fog. Tell her
caramelized onion and marionberry noon hoodie."
Levinas interrupts and puts Buber in a half-nelson.
"Just say here," he insists. "Here am I, send me."
O am I derailed by mystical thinking, and flung to lay
among what past had only been the view. I missed
the course on whatever kind of gratitude makes
one practical. All I do is rest in train shadow.
Here between the crosses and the scrub burrs,
I memorize temperatures. I want to be a human tilde.
Here I wait to call. Here I wait in total breath to give.

Oh No: That's So Cool

'Oh, to be in Los Angeles, and not have a car!' —
Nancy Wang, from Jordaan Mason's Facebook wall

Yet I still can't believe how strange it is to be
anything: how strange to be oranges, ReMax,
line splitters, all the overcooked tomatoes.
Who ganked their metaphors from commercials?
Not me. How strange to be easy to follow!
You wake up one day and there is a city
named after you. Let me see your to-do list.
How strange this intermission music or giving
in. To be the last olive, the first biplane.
I want to reincarnate as an emotional guitar solo:
the same people will like me or not like me, I
think. Death: your candygram is here from Sure.
How strange the scout ant, the stranger with
news, the rotunda and the racist joke. Well,
bold! It's bold to unify any of it, and if you
can, that's good. That's pretty good. That's
okay. How strange to think about the painting
done. Will it be? How many the bees. How often
the seat outgrown. How lazy the drain. You
know something I don't, I bet. I bet. I throw
in and take from and try through and need even
you, rushing off with a bucket of something,
with that haircut I will like but never get.

I Am Enjoying These Limits, He Said to the Waitress

Someone near the river (who will
not be introduced by occupation)
is annotating every dip of finch
with a system of phone strokes:

7 S 7 _ 7 S 7 _ 7 3 7 _ 7

Model airplanes near the Kodak plant.
Innertubes for salvage. A fence
with poison oak in the gaps,
a route to the sheriff's
election billboard.

We have paint thinner.
Slogans!

We take our burritos and codeine
down to the action figure expo.

Outside, skaters guzzle NyQuil
and grind rails and blow hint-of
cherry soap bubbles out of
yellow wands.

You know, we will need to
shoo the hangers-on,
the brats of peanut butter knees
doing pull-ups on our awning bars
for some contest. For their
application. Soon. Okay?

This is a green, green bridge,
and this is a train, train trestle,
and these are the old, old
Vans. Punks in the beerlight,
mythologies in the lip rings.

This is what we call
radio silence.

Mama Told You Not to Come

I am not the hitchhiker to end all hitchhikers.
The bus stranded me in Crescent City, California
with a MySpace account and charisma brochure.
Now I am full of total reality goals. No shit.
S. scrambles eggs and hemlock. She is, you know,
a "shawl girl." M. solders flower urns for the set of
Martha Stewart Living. What? A living. It's called
living. With heirloom mugs, hobbies straight off
slow movies, wet-one-today-eh, gas station X-
mas lights. Over here! We are careful as hell.

This is not the town to end all towns. Please:
replace the hammers with hand-shaped hammers.
Town. Tow truck. Trowel. Travis fries bacon all
night. Travis is a father. Travis? Are you up?
You are just the sort of Travis we expected.
Over here! You, who are a father. Who, once,
was not a NASCAR matador? We hugged nickels.
We threw pshaw at the cardboard. One specific
beard washes up on shore and then some. Send
helicopters to drag the ocean for the culprit.
Please save us from this beard! Danger: stranger
hair. Last seen in mackinaws and torn belts.
Plus on Ferris wheels, a thumb out for that blue
ride. Be kind to the sketch artist. He's dead.

What Do You Owe Your Zip Code?

Hey, no smoking
on the go-karts.

We skid stopped past the
off ramp to browse this van:

a cult's old blankets
and off-season Clementines.

That's nice, that bracelet
jingles like a dancer caught

her ankle in the algae.
She is a Viking slave.

Take now, a night hiss,
a slur of proud-ass barns

and the crooked tickle
of satellite dishes.

Squint for rainy promises
or the rainy promenades

that never go down.
Oh, this is no cello analogy

you weepy motherfucker.
These parking lots

are places to park.
Issac sells safety

razors in the arcade tent.
You might try to barter

with a fist full of
swallows. Let me say

this just this once:
That's a long ass way

from a deal.

The Local Pompadour

Lamp cord in a coma: I know, I know! It's
strenuous to shepherd electricity. Believe
much? Don't. You are causing electric
delays. Your nancy boat takes too long.
We have major bass tournaments and dead
tourist trap whitewater rafting to organize.
All these things scarf electricity. Augusta's
traditional greens are kept tidy thanks to
spacemen. Spacemen in their wee space boots
skate around underneath the greens with lanterns
to keep the greens soft, warm, comfortable, a tad
lickable. The greens understand. The greens con-
sult the local horoscope. For seventeen days, local
horoscope maestro I was, memorizing birthdays
of friends, allowing petty feuds to rule the fates of
dozens. It was a small town. We fished. We had no
complimentary doughnuts. The revitalization scarecrows
gabbed plans of toll-free phone numbers and Hug It
Out sessions. One scarecrow wrote a book called
The Fucked Chevrolet: A Tough Pastoral Stance.
One scarecrow wired up a lantern in his chest.
He called his heart matter a kind of mine.
Where is my outlet, he is fond of saying, all
down the day, all down these streets, these
streets of little to no to tons of rain.

for Kasey

The Missionary Positron

is the name of a personal ark
christened by a lava lamp
and Calvinist by discretion
which means empty. We all
drowned. Inside, there are ovens
full of cushions and lightbulbs
illustrated with Bible scenes.
Thousands of jackets but no
buttons. Instead of blinds,
power strips. Everything is dark
except now and then a pink light
strobes the floor like a cockroach.
All the bedrooms smell like licorice.
The shower spits wriggles of paper,
each one offering a clever reason
for the last. Everyone you love is
represented by their thumbprints on
silverware, none of which is ever
washed but soaks eternally in buckets
hidden around like Easter eggs even the
parents forgot about. Open the fridge:
it's just frozen latkes arranged to spell
the time. Each room is through a room's
fireplace, so maybe it's a good thing
we're dead already, right? You're right:
sometimes I think of my brain as a
coked out deli manager, running around
with pumpernickel and ham in a juggle,
screaming BE MORE RADICAL! at the
sandwich artists. Life is a lot of
clarification and limited-time options
which is why it's good to listen to
real people and turn everything they say

into a family of origami frogs and hide
under that person's bed, arranging frogs
forever and letting worry do its heavy thing
like some kind of mega dumbfuck at the helm.

for Jason

We Are Just Bells
in the Soup Nazi's Dream

and play that "who can be the more audacious
dumb." Yet these swamp minnow years made me
so cheap, lies I tell on trains don't even
sting. What else? Well, the strip mall
is still a neighborhood, full of busy
bodies, where the mattress saleswoman
watches football in the Dominos forever,
up until a 4th and 13 punt arcs up and up and
hits her, jaw-abouts, shattering a strudel of
brain that slipped there when she was
seventeen, hot shit behind a Spearmint veil
and faking hip drawls for branchwater (which
sounds a lot more badass than it tastes),
hiding from the bouncer with quarter
after quarter into the bull's lever.
Ride on O someone's little sister!

But, that extra brain so dislodged,
she is free to quit the mattress factory
(keep up, please) and sue and lose
to a technicality with a combover
who checks Craigslist every weekend
for Soviet telescopes. They marry
in the laundromat, splurge for a
Nickelback cover band, and delay vows
while the drummer's cigarette break
is besieged by high collared visions
commanding that he relapse into tractor
something something and an ulcer-shaped
duty to hold his hat at that tummy level
bespeaking a solid dearth of hubris,
then sobergulp his way Back To Town
and fess up his ledger: a daughter,

curious! Her Minny Mouse eyeglasses chip
when she pirouettes off the swing and heave
-ho's: she can't find them or remember to
cry, what with this fine all—limes!
the White House!—turning a cautiously
awesome red all of a sudden, the color of
when a glass Coke bottle mouth is blown across.
I will give you a second if you need it.
Then your own daughter calls to say
her own daughter's learned in school today
the names of bones, eighty-odd, new ones that
Science just invented. Why, she even
knows how to swim now without holding
everybody's breath. Isn't that everything?
You are now a lot more cool than before.

for Ashland

Blue Wheels and Handshakes

We spill like the doughnuts of best boys
at work on a light fixture commercial.

Jay curls rinds of duct-tape around
the lever that lifts his footstool.
Mr. Shingle steps unsaluted by the
cab driver from the green rail to the trout molars.
Andrew repairs the Keno machines
and keeps some toothpaste in his glovebox.

Chris bought a cloak of liquid silver and
sidesteps the anthill outside the library.
Frank hid in a daguerreotype of a rowboat
then sicced the sparrows on his own ribcage.
I run into a janitor I know outside of Denny's.
He wails for vinegar chips from the cape.

Ross rode a coastline that slurs your
tongue hair on a bus down from Seattle,
but steering back up (twenty years gone)
sees now the absence of ice cream shops.

Daniel gawks through life at Chuckie Cheese,
drives a van and owns a full-hilt saber,
none of which will stop Doritos
from mangling their bag design.

"They've gone all star white," he says to me.
And, "I want to sell the notions of May on eBay."
And, "Where are you these days, you fucker? Around
here, we're stuck with squirt guns in the belly swamps."

And I remember watching two men shrug
on a public bus, mustaches twenty years stale,
after discussing nothing less than shame,
what damns a shame and demands from us—

And I can still say Bill, Bill, cabbie Bill
(his beard like bread heels for seagulls)
who drove my mother to my birth—
he would have kept track of Mr. Shingle's ride
from the Motel 6 to the green bridge,
and here should go a million pump organs!

O we are armed with eyelashes and WD-40
and how our denim only kids the fall.
So what is my love with these shot pipes,
with these new regulations for toilets?

Some of us want to see New Zealand.
Some of us have astronaut Kool-Aid mugs.
And some of us are only happy in the snow,
trying on all of the lost white gloves.

What I've Learned
From Sleeping in New England

Studies have shown that only the sleep deprived will
sleep with me. My housemate just mentioned a velvet
dick: maybe that's the standard we're working under?
But I look upon your petrified daughters of the revolution
forest, your barns of Vermont with mallard animations
sponsored by all-things-will-pass.com, your gorges and
sweet corn, thunderstorms and chimney ingenuity,
your Presidential asparagus and miles of stone,
maple ice cream, scholarships and flannel sunsets,
wheat league baseball and weak kneed scholars,
your fifteen dollar demolition derby tickets and two
fingered prayers, blueberry marshes and cabbage malls,
hypothetical dance crazes post-Liberal victory, your pet
yawns, your house walrus, your imitation of the walrus
yawn, your cell phone chargers and giant mums, all the
Appleseed cousins agape in the Connecticut with hacksaws for
medicine, all the sisters of former Energy Secretaries in
progressive high school theatres and coffeeshop divorce trials,
your decent mileage versus your snow tires versus your
bicycle endorsement, theoretically, for others—"hey,
wait, I own seven bicycles, they're on Craigslist"—
your three dollar avocados and great advancements in
emotional theory, your Thishampton and Thathampton,
your one exit to Fenway Park and your legitimate fear of
hugs—don't worry, I'm not going to hug you, I'm an
intellectual—your byzantine Pike and moose and trains,
your girls of interesting tattoos such as powerlines,
the way your long winters crimp even Santa to liquor,
your grave, dark haired feminist boys who tow the good ship
Beard Trimmer from one sullen hook up to another, who lazily
graze on their own fuck ups and network in the shower,
who in lieu of pecans will toast your pumpkin seeds,
that being a kind of sexual innuendo I won't explain,

not in the face of your expensive research and cheap
buses, not without a draft from your snowplow driver's
early bourbon, not unless I'm allowed to debut the great
Hawaiian shirt of my intuition that suggests I call your
bullshit. Nope! For now I look upon your Hudson River
School dream innovations as an invitation to my own
entitlement, the backwards Pac Man of American Destiny
that I will do my hella best to manifest upon your shore.
In the kitchen of your renovated mill. In the basement
of an all-girls college dorm and how we're not endearing
back and forth, New England, since we're neither of us
mulberry hedges sheared toward a clever apology or
a petition to keep cocaine out of our vulnerable sunsets
and deep under the minus twenty degree snow drifts of
April where it so belongs and might lead a Hampshire grad
guilty on the bacon of Derridean blowjobs to go, "I'm
tough, I know why wheat bread is better and why white bread
tricked everybody after the Great Depression, ready to say
'Hey, thanks for the footstool.' And so I announce my
intentions to announce New Hampshire's New Man in the Mtn!"
Which they really will build; I'm not saying they won't.
I'm not offending you on purpose by asking to see your
tattoo, it's just I'm curious, some curious hick on the
back of a condor all the way here from a cheap place
like Reno, the Reno in your head I mean, because I really
dig your heads and all the different little heads under
wool here. They're the evolution of heads, I think.
I look upon your heads and your thin legs built of some
cigarette / asparagus hybrid with zero emissions not
frozen like me in this stupid leather jacket and I think,
"Dear Entitlement, I'm not asleep yet. Give me your
smallpox lecture. Everyone should have sex on Emily
Dickinson's grave is my theory, and if you need a
ticket man, I'll be him, or a new pronoun! I'm almost
not kidding. Home is not just where to bed an easy love.
The home should always look a little like it's dead."

Eat This City! Eat This City Oh

No, not "home" you haven't even bought
a real lamp. Friends you tell them all of
flesh and local compromise, this act is
act this, ignore that, silly rabbit:
you are not where I reach at in sleep.
I sign birthday cards on the night bus.
Sundays I jar the apple mash for Bea.
When you say always with the fucking
apples, you mean: "Bea? Listen. On you
he stews so much that he cuds this new
love. Chews later. Who does that shit!
Love has a half life and molders in there.
It's science." But so we go, each among the
other, a game of open hand demand, with
marbles suspected beneath the skin.
We suspect sex on a train in the woods.
Maybe a bad call, a drunk walk in April snow,
a boxing match to story up the scar you
won't. What want do you hoist and schlep
to town? What will you bet? This, he says,
and scoots across a tin of yellow mints.
Okay? We lift our cards, avoid the tell.
We try to guess whatever look we share.

Eh Is Right

Drop me off first. Then spend the night
in the parking lot of the funeral home
where two of these men dropped a casket
almost, got it back up, then high-fived.
Amateur opera singers do their own makeup.
The higher you go, the more your face gets
installed. Then it dries and waits for your
approval. I keep getting submitted to
withdrawal. We all say things none of us
believe, like "gift economy." Or "wait."
Each surface is buffed by the quality of
sleep available there. Certain people you
care about and then I care about you
a lot more. Antique vendors swarm the
house for what the significant didn't want.
The owner of a go-kart track urges his
friends to help him build a fire-resistant
tower around everything he loves, which was
not the original plan. "Make it about more
than one thing," I told you, and then you
told me I told you, and I felt stupid.
The fireman pours shampoo on a robin
and washes it up in his red bucket hat.
Tell me how you really feel and if it
helps, I'll pretend that you're asleep.

We Are All Good
If They Try Hard Enough

No, I am not out to start a smear campaign.
For you who you are and stuff you're good,
ripcord! When I grow up, I want to be
patience, an asterisk, or the kitchen when
"I'm not trying to be an ass but honestly"
is frying and frying his cardigan to chase the
New Real. Us mood thieves, weren't we
not invited? Why are we going off about
snot bouts, hey ho, no way, the sigh dial,
like the first rule of polite company is
don't talk about polite company. I really
hate it here, which is such a stretch.
Strong feelings, I mean. I never got
buzzed in to those. I take a Z-shaped
fire escape up to the hospital of feeling.
What an anti-ripcord sort of beauty that Z!
And I stroll on up whenever it is I consider
you. For some reason, right now, I want to
love you in what they're saying is orange
and endless, honestly. Shrug. How's it feel
to weigh that much in news? Orange and
endless. That's good for what it is, I
guess. If you're sure you are, I trust you.

A Sample of Your New Luck

Neither of us signed up for this scrutiny,
bear-soft and set to club the hive
both. We never read the instructions
on this cream. We bought the tin
for the tap of our nails against, and to
trim them is the lonely opposite of
gross. Darling, when did we walk into
suction cups and the release forms of
a sleep study that jolts us *huh* to hear
"Congratulations!" up the hall, but for
who? Did you catch that? Now we're
happy for them? Oh. We've heard tell
of Accomplishments like get-you-some,
so we staple on dead ant mustaches and,
like, is that what you mean? Will someone
knock on our pillow tonight to say, "Howdy,
you've won! It's over! These side bets,
a battalion of 7s, the holy escalator,
plum juice atomized, a dessert collage
from checkered flags and FDR's diary:
this is but a sample of your new luck."
All of these I stow in my chest bones
like Christmas presents that embarrass
airport security and make them think,
"Either I gave shitty things this year
or got some. Why can't I remember?"
The night is a commercial for trains.
Dreams on call with eyebrows wet.
I'm making a lot of money counting
how awake I can stay in the tyranny of
sequels to self-recipes. Should I practice
my headers? Did I cauterize my friend?
You're rubbing the cream mask in your

fit, all over the cool side. Eighty-six
umbrellas open in the street, and they
spell something in how they float (is it
a billet-doux?) NO, THE INSTRUCTIONS SAY
RUB IN GENTLY. THEY NEVER SAID MASK.

Belief Is a Long Smoke to Come

What's neat about a leader is they never sleep.
They scout for small miracles of providence,
asparagus for breakfast, rosemary for anti-coma
tricks. Leaders, they are everybody's security
breath, hymns in the bullhorns. Scared on the wrong
end of the elevator accident hotline, they fed me
prophecies of redwoods felled under butter knives
and the new machine that makes change regular as
folk. They showed me a trough full of toothpaste.
Listen, they said, we now enter the famous time of
situation. You'll burn your lease for soy compost.
Documentaries will arise of the new milk truck races,
and all the networks will ask if we can play ourselves.
You will enter, they said, the famous role of the
hurricane reporter. Central air will slow to hand fans.
Camels will race like awkward teenaged point guards.
Liars will sell back your reflection in the duct tape.
The leaders were so frank! I thanked them in advance.
Elevator escape occurred, and I matured by an
offramp in Maine, selling mugs, unicorn blankets,
mandarins and how-not-to manuals. Now I dream of
incremental collapse and can't tell it apart from
sleeping till noon. O someone with a lot of sheep go
bless those leaders with their situation heads, barking
hope's famous gristle and directions to all the fun-
damental loneliness we were already pretty good at.
Networks, give us what we're here to want: leaders,
seated on the chair's very edge, one finger all *shush,*
as they try again to light a match against a firefly.

   for Barack

The Man Alone at Cumberland Farms the Other Night Who Bought Milano Cookies With a $20 Bill

Will he read this? Are you warm yet?
If he doesn't, will you tie me to a
sheepdog who will never brag that he's
"people watching, you know. I don't get
bored: I'm a people watcher." Wrong.
In 1954, the last documented case of
"real people" buried a milkshake recipe
and two coupons for used boxing gloves
outside Sparks, Nevada. Don't have a fit.
No points to win from me, I'm afraid.
I'm so afraid of overdoing it, always.
Like this. This is just for more friends.
Ten to my keychain, six to my Rub List.
We'll raid something. Grade movies. Bowl.
Chuck carrier pigeons down the tunnel:
"Hi! Hi back! Hi back back! Yum, the
sun is a little jealous. He's not a
secret, like our handshake spark."
You're my friend because you're not
"I'm a person"–this and "I'm real"–that.
You'll never demand I check you for lumps
or call me on behalf of some hallelujah
screw. You'll never stuff a prairie dog
in my freezer with a note: LUV U MIKE!!!
This army of ours, this army of ours.
I know what you're thinking and yes,
you can. Step one: Is it dawn yet?
Is that chocolate? Are you cold?

Mindy the Famous Divebomber Visits the Thrift Store We All Care For

Mindy the famous divebomber
took her blazer to very sincere
dry cleaners. Then things began to
snow, of course, which made her
stalwart. She went to the thrift
store to buy a hooded blazer.
Shut up. I know they don't. It's
a poem. Mindy, the divebomber,
cavorts, digs among the Slim Jim
30th Anniversary t-shirts and
pleated trousers, wigs and old men
thumbing the gunslinger pulp.
Did you know Egyptians invented
paper? I am a public education system.
Did you know we are run mostly by
hospitals? Mindy digs past Mother of
Ketchup and Macaroni Salad who
dances a little in a swell dress.
See? We are fine, after all.
Her child is not quite convinced.
Where are all the lights? Why are you
apologizing? I want a hooded blazer.
Mindy, the famous divebomber, situation
mingle, high alert. Where is your chute
of rockabilly gumption? A soldier never
lies, famous Mindy. Who do you get to
die on? Yes, in an ill-fitted blazer. But
it's only fifty cents. The transaction
is witnessed by a tour group.
They are up in arms, giggles.
They are here to define us.

In Case You Were Wondering

You got mustard all over.
Careful, or you melt into
the old drunk of flinches
who promises promises,
saddles up and whispers
how he hung his white
blazer on a sure thing
in a May apartment. This,
then his rest cure is over.
He knows maybe of a girl
who sold his legal name.
Gone back for it with
a discount magnet and
know how to hold it right
on in over there. That's the
spot. Sweet, too. Well,
once, sweet on some of
us, famous as sagebrush,
the jerry-rigged scenery
of our commiserate theatre.
Who is he talking to? Like
Tootsie Pops: the world may
never and so forth. The sun
sets in the Utah desert like
a stranger who knows what you
did but lets you, waves you on.

> *for Chris*

Now You Try

Your roommate has something to tell you about the sociology of chip brands. Driving has something to tell you about shivering. Your porch has something to tell you about your ex-girlfriend. Evolution has something to tell you about acne. Bea Arthur has something to tell you about drugs. Beaches have something to tell you about community. Your mom has something to tell you, sometimes. The post office has something to tell you about the rest of your life. Coffee has something to tell you but can't remember. Sleep has something to tell you about accommodation. Snacks have something to tell you about waiting. Field goals in the red zone have something to tell you about what you should think of "satisfaction." The Internet has the sum of things to tell you. Sunglasses have something to tell you about sex. Corn fritters have something to tell you about ambition. Fog has something to tell you about your heart, but only at certain hours. Breathing has something to tell you about children. You have something to tell me you won't. The chef has something to tell you about liaisons. Strangers have something to tell you about your mood. Love has the only thing to tell you about love. Make your lover tell you something about something you do in your sleep. Boredom has something to tell you about accumulation. Whenever God has something to tell you about a particular area, an exclamation point will show up in the lower-left corner of your screen. Barry Bonds has something to tell you about fighting AIDS, but this is just something I heard. First science has something to tell you about petting. Then science had something to tell you about petting. Petting has nothing to tell you about science. Petting does have something to tell you about guessing. Malls have something to tell you about Christmas. VCR technology has something to tell you about Republicans. A good thing is something that has something to tell you about something. If you are lying in bed and there is a maple bonbon on your nightstand a little out of reach, how much and what kind of effort you employ through your body toward that bonbon has something to tell you about death. 4AM has something to tell you, but it's outside. The press has something to tell you they saw, but they always wait until it's gone. Watermelons have something smart to tell you. Breakfast has something to tell you about your friends. The Decemberists have something to tell you about Russian history—yeah, you and everybody else, dude. Dreams have something to tell you about where to swim. Movie trailers have something to tell you about what you want. M&Ms have something to tell you about your next thought. Dancing has something to tell you about worry. Cussing has something to tell you about instructions. Fights between hockey goalies have something men don't tell you. If you have something to tell me, come here. Money has something to tell you about not sleeping. What I told you was something I meant to mean something about something I had to tell you about. Knowing has something to tell you about politics. Rain has something to tell you about blame. Fruit flies have something to tell you about residency. Tollbooths have something to tell you about cameras. Tell-all's sell something to have. We always have something to tell the dictionary. Please listen I have something to tell you. Please tell me I have something. Toothbrushes have something to tell you about your sense of humor. Having tells something to use you. Your head has something to tell you about scarecrows. There's someone here for you. Do you want me to tell them to go home?

The Trip All Whoppyjawed

I was going to bike to Cumberland Farms and buy
eggs, but my bike doesn't work. The end of the
joke is "and I don't like eggs," which is

bullshit. I love eggs. Emma S, you said my last
breakfast poem had like an overdose of "breakfast
this, breakfast that—okay, we get it." So just

eggs. Jupiter eggs. Eggs in a musket barrel.
Eggs with New Jersey tans. Eggs on an all-
expenses paid vacation to *Lick That Lick!*

(Emma: please suicide-by-cop the bad lines.
Anything short of an emotional Tang-shot.
If it doesn't hit a bird with its pitch: cut.

It's on you, girl. I've really invested a lot in this
"bad boy," so let's not go and make a frat initiation
causality of a fine young poem like myself, like all my

friends! I've got so many poem friends. They all
sexy as pine needles and obsessed with Indian
reparations as a metaphor for "bad party gifts.")

Eggs white people like. Eggs in a sad cartoon,
but only in cameos for the unfazed to hunt, like
"Look! There's one by that cancer slut's hammock!"

I'm not worried at all. She's got a Will to live
for. He played Wesley on *Star Trek* and he's always
meaning things and thinking about when to mean next.

I was going to bike to Cumberland Farms and buy
anything at all that would feel like an asterisk
looks by itself on a page by itself at night.

My Heart Is a Small Yellow Emoticon Wearing a Cowboy Hat in the Snow

Are there music videos in sign language?
No, I mean, is there a whole thing for them?

My heart quit to get a job selling ice machines.
On receipts he writes, like, "Don't be swayed,

sway!" He is one to give of himself. Once he found each
happy person in an alley between two brownstones.

They were spread around in beach chairs,
picking the glass out of their teeth.

With him gone, I've taken to drawing different lights
for the same face: deli aisle, arctic dawn, old silo.

It turns out there's a whole thing for us.
I log in and ascertain of many. What's great

is when someone who hasn't changed in a while
updates. Also, there are a lot of words for the same

person, like douchebag, lava expert, and Boo.
There is the snow I can lick off my knuckles,

but then the way of my feelings by you,
as if a small kitchen person were called

by you, told to open the stove, and found
a breakfast nook. Then, of course, other things

which mostly I enjoy, the lay of those I know,
anyway, from the letters that my heart sends back.

Tell Me and I Will Know

Most of my time is spent displacing want.
In some of it, the water heater's bugged.

When I turn my face under the cold kind,
what I'm trying to do is divorce my head.

I am most proud of my existential friends
and secretly embarrassed by sweet weather.

We follow the road back to the missed exit.
That is the worst mood I can think of.

My moments of inward congratulation are
offset by meals alone in pants I really like.

There is a harmonica under the river.
There is the time we kiss our own wrist.

Now I have talked my way through dawn
and then some, hot up with promises.

No longer do I pack my own face towel.
Trust lives by its own impossibility.

One girl sat in the shopping cart, almost
asleep. Her friend didn't know what to say.

There are things you keep dust off.
There is no way to explain this.

What they don't tell you about God
is that it waits for one kind of laughter

to appear in two people at once.
This has never happened. Wait.

Downstream stood another set of bathers.
We felt like someone was writing a song.

Give me something to give into.
It will be weird. It will be so weird.

for Lindsay

Don't Wake Up It's Just Me

If I know exactly what you mean,
will we both fit on the motorcycle?
If I say streetlight, will you say
half-in, half-out? If I say pumpkin stew,
will you say ghost flesh? Writ large and
quivering on a blimp, beep beep, the
antithesis of confession. I want to
advertise. I want you to come in and
sip, sit, scorn with me. Do stillwater
strokes and will the knuckles to pop.
Wait, I know exactly what you mean.
Let's try out tender vessels: they're
on sale. Join to the point of collapse
into. Accordion honk flesh. Oh. Oh.
If I say streetlight, you say back in.
And if I say dumpster diving, you say
chocolate factory. If I know exactly
when to wake up, you know how to stay
nervous, somewhere else, breathing, mum-
bling. Is this a trick? What game do you win
with trust? The word okay is like skydiving.
If I say swingsets, will you make it rain?

Lovesong With Civic Responsibility

We could hotwire this blood drive van
and never feel too slow for our hearts.
This kind of thing has precedents, even
balloons and sanitary tape. Your horse
Pumpkin can ride too if she shaves the
act off, swims back up the womb of the
respectable. You know, turns into a
local sports anchor. "This is Pumpkin,
reporting at a yellow. Wowee, look, I'm
biased. I've served caution its tea
and all I've won is my beach shadow
makes it to the water and I don't."
Blood drive van plows into ice cream
museum, blood drive pirates ransack
Peter Pans to New York for cheap
dates. Blood drive revolutionaries
blip bloop across the CIA's map of
Levels of Concern Below "Hooker Riot."
Drip goes our siren. When all this dies
fondly, they'll have to establish some
holiday. Kids will vaguely herald
Pumpkin on Mondays off, as they
rip new xylophone tricks and mud
tickle. No, I don't know what kids *oh
my God* about these days or if my arm's
purple blotches need more serious
care than what I have, right now,
in your gurney of positive O.

Strike While the Iron is Made of Real People

O my new spell and what the heck,
call it ours. Tell your co-star that
selfishness ruins hugs. Compromise the
glass and publicize the ice, don't let
shootouts be such a secret time.
Like this woman who is neighborly
enough was arrested for menagerie
infractions and watched, restrained,
as her oxen, does, happy snakes,
and lagoon shaped ostriches got
warded to the state. "Don't take
my rams!" she said. "Not— please."
I feel airborne for everyone. Yeah.
Make my subscriptions all known up. Love
hides on the line, hand over mouthpiece.
Cake is only if you share out to the disco.
You can remember like this: shellfish
ruin the water supply. Shellfish etc.
When a lot of people love each other,
shower curtains start to feel like who
are you kidding in there? Heed the fable
of Salyut 7: the commander spent hours
alone, staring out of portholes. And lo,
the whole galaxy folded up into a yellow tilde.
But now, a commission has wrought
a pep hock: Go Home If Space Is That Bad,
to make us like, "Oh yeah, the aberration of
sadness, roger." And so now to sleep with
the commander in the spirit of let's-all-
need-together, and he doesn't know, like
you do, about this microphone under my lip.

Money

Most of the people who had money still do.
Things amuse them and make them curious.
They have time for all of these things.
They are practical and have maybe gone to
another country. They are trying to be
right by what's around and not an asshole
maybe. They are nice and amused a lot and
raunchy which is nice and amusing like
wow, hahahahaha, I get it. I bought it.
One day they are like hey, we're pretty
good at stuff and funny and maybe a little
beautiful, let's start a poetry magazine.
Or whatever. They are amusing. They are
smart. They know that being amusing is
good because it makes you feel good and
feeling is everything and maybe, okay,
let's be honest, sometimes they feel
anxious and that the world is a lot
ridiculous, like totally not amusing
though, but just really fucked, yeah,
which they know because they're smart
and know at stuff and have maybe gone
to another country and they have money.
So they're like let's be amusing and feel
good and feel each other and feel what's
amusing until we are a little still or a
lot. I think that's all of it for them.
And then there are other people who—
right. Exactly. Or they have money but
something really terrible and shitty
and fucked happened to them that was not
the world but was something more by which
I mean closer. These people are embarrassing.

It's like I have never felt as bad as them
and I feel bad feeling good but still not
bad enough. They are laughing a little which
is good, right? Which means they feel good?
Good. Feeling good is good. Money is good.
Amusing is good. Know is good. Smart is good.
Whatever is good. Wow is good. Hey is good.
Country is good. Beautiful is good. Start is good.
Good is good. Good good funny person:
is it terrible to feel like I always have?

Instead of Taking a Shower

I

I have two moods: cruel or nervous.
And a vial of infectious ha-ha-ha.
They printed all the riddles without
reward money. Affection last seen
clamped or camp. I'm a gully in the
steam of your sidewalk accordion.
If that's hard to follow, I'm right
behind you. Time's got a top-notch
immune system. Just now, I grew my
beard toward a show of support.
Sure, you have your own life's blue
deed, but I have a satellite's habit.

II

Look! All those ideas wanted tailors.
Which means I am programmed to omit
cannoli, Elvis, a flashlight in a boot,
shipwrights, the two breasts on the
matchbook Nicole drew for me (breasts
not the matchbook) the glory morning
train (the song not the train)—well,
shit, it's all an idea, I guess. You
are a combination impossible to press
in chorus. Both the peekaboo and long
kinds of need. This is your medal.
This is also a heretofore uncharted
mood named Kitten in a Cedar, named
Chicory and Whiskey. Three moods, I
guess: cruel, nervous, and love poem.

The Relevant Oh

You need to sneak behind your life and bite it
gently on the shoulder. Let mutual friends label
mutual friends in ways uncomfortably direct.
Mimic what another person's face might be doing
in front of them. Did you take another shower?
Your multivitamin? Advantage of the calendar?
The new meditation knights each experience.
Out to avoid power, we apologize with style.
Curlicues of breath propel the "fuck it" into
plan. Saturday I wanted a pompadour and a ride,
now I just want to tell you about the biscuit,
how parts of me always want to hug butter
and scream, "Let it alone! Stop assembling
and membering and sleep in jambalaya!"
But my audience is under architecture. They
break the fingernail clippers and fix them.
They're full of recipes and sacred digits.
What you know is I don't even consider my
skin mine. So you try to explain at me how it
tastes, then you uncurl my fingers toward five
maneuvers that have always worked with you.

The Difference Between Art and Play

Sometimes I think I can only love the joke
because how else to all of us at once like oh!
and then how this tarantula of mirth claws
through our guts and does its tickle best,
even growing new arms for the slow or shy.
Is it the tiny death in laughing that I love or the
silence out? Well, is it friends or audience?
Learning that anything can be a service animal,
like you can get a bat if your disability is Not
Scary Enough, you find a person and you hold
a pane of glass up and ask them to kiss it then
you. Now, yes, they make a Venn diagram.
And they list all of the things they love, but
they do it in a language you don't seem to have.

for Elliot & Erin & Marcus & Patrick (& Nora)

Your Forever Shake and You

There's something wrong with a voice.
How any word is just your air massaged,
whether you compliment a new scarf
or read a son's name off a telegram.
How we borrowed the command for quiet
from wind, so when people say *shhhh*
what they want is for you to feel cold.
How, when caught by light, we shut up.
What any voice is out to say is *wait,*
over here. And once they can see you,
who cares to make sure they heard right?
Still, you turn up the jar boy's wail.
You shout *goddammit* to the white
out on the freeway. The phatic function
of language changes like taste in rhythm,
so the parents go *If, gee, say, a zebra*
and my girlfriend says *It's all like, like*
calumniation of original intent and shit.
She's right. Praise is no more than a
pinfeather and prayer has no color but
a space for color. All enough to make you
feel silly ordering people to feel better
and too self-conscious for long distance sex.
But there you hark. Stalk. Hock up enough
phlegm to spit out *no, that's not what I*
meant. And then you talk about headless
girls naked and asleep in a fleece of pine sap,
or the price of Milk Duds, how you made out
with a cottonmouth bite, precious instructions
to barbers and pepper wielders, all your opinions
on all of the sky's insurmountable whims.
You plead and cavort and joke and affirm

and lecture and mewl and bray and slip in
and warn and cheer and clarify and say
good night which means *I want to be alive
more and I want part of that life to be with
you.* You look out over the crowd and say
Thank you, it's really great to be here!
which really means it's great to say
what you've made to say, like to say
*The sentence is a house of language
that wants to be such a good home
no word ever leaves.* But everything
lives, if it can. You scream a name and
creekbeds answer. You learn to go
hum down the sidewalk just for you.
Whatever you do, you don't interrupt the
phonebooth band. In parkas and shoeless,
the members hunch all over town with strings
of digits, and they whisper *come on now.*
They listen for someone to hear them.
Most of what they do is tap on things.

   for Matt

Let's Hear It Over Here

Let's hear it for the half-awake
fauxhawks of the honest naked.

Sleeping on the pillow end feels of
drowning in a vat of cookie dough.

Eating new cereal reminds of parkas. Smoke:
of camper shells on the lakebed, dogs about.

Let's shadowbox the snow!
Let's dress in tissues and cat tails!

Hmm. Half-awake with dandruff teeth.
Steam turtlenecks our brains.

Let's resolve to automate sincerity
in this age of telepathic iPods.

Let's hear it for those of us
who are never in the loop like that.

Who are still taping up old ornaments
and alphabetizing home movies by flashlight.

Who are at it with our pockets and large,
clumsy tips. We didn't mean it that way.

Who smile at first glance to mannequins,
and at second, and so on, snowed on

and snowed on, and sewed wrong, snowed on
and thrown off, and so long, kiddo.

Sleep and do right by. Would you even
be here if we hadn't come for you?

Me and My Friends Have Sarcastic Beards

I don't trust kids my age who don't have Friends In the War,
are into war, render war, END DA WAR! Excuse me, you look
real-ish: did we go to Sarah Lawrence and protest something?
You make me feel like a logger on a spaceship. Like I wash my
hair too much. Like my eyes should grow to accommodate these
white sunglasses. Raybands? I make up weekday drinking names
outside The Basement with a girl who schools me on Brian Wilson.
O if we could sack fossil fuels for your discography trivia.
It's not like I want something "holy" or I find the prim and
lonely Visigoths. It's just a meth versus coke kind of thing.
A mail order Neutral Milk Hotel shirt versus a concert stain.
You make me feel like if I gave you a tree frog, it would die
on Monday but receive abundant mention in your MySpace survey.
You make me feel like using the stove to light a cigarette is a
photo op. Wait, you have a bank account set aside for laser
tattoo removal, but maybe I forgot to click Remember Me.
"No, I was in Berlin reading Nietzsche and accelerating the
boob to aporia ratio." "As of late, I have been totally loving
Tropicana—wait—trip to Kenya?—no, no, tropicália. Tom Ze."
It's not like I want something "hash brown" or I don't find
Beautiful Losers recitation skillz essential. Excuse me.
Not when there is white denim to revive, not when bottle
necks still make for good slide guitar, not when you blinged out
the dead tree frog, not when you bought a free trade
plunger, not when we sang all night in a Sarah Lawrence loft
until Eoin pissed on your cell phone charger and solved
racism, bisexuality, and how to court a zesty violent twee.
Remember when I got all up in your shit and you fed my
email address to those porn websites? I feel like a boy
made of old man socks and very clever text messages.
Joe Cook's knuckles exploded in the desert. God you luv and
fuck your world. Just kidding about God. Who is Joe Cook?

Did he go to Sarah Lawrence and protest something?
Remember when you told me I should fuck that girl,
then you wrote "make love" in your poem? So did I. Amen.

for Northampton

Global Widespread Panic

And there was no global widespread Ativan.
This was a look-at-my-face-does-it-look-
gotcha-it-doesn't-look-gotcha-it-looks-
oh-shit kind of deal. Woe usurped the
deeds. Snakes ate the food stamps.
God's wheelchair hit a baby sapling.
Not even a nice shower felt that nice.
UN officials took to wearing charcoal
baseball makeup. We set the laundromats
on fire, by which I mean OMG LAUNDROMAT
PARTY! We didn't worry about having grand
kids or copies of The Lion King for
them. Nobody invented new aftershaves.
No history was coveted, not even by the
apologists or for marketing purposes.
When Shasta Lake went dry, we held a
contest: EMERGENCY REFILL IDOL™
The winners: iced coffee, Dr. Pepper,
benzyl peroxide, breast milk, and Tang.
Plenty of disgruntled cum jockeys felt
left out, which didn't seem, you know,
"shocking." If by this point you're like,
"wait a minute what about eternal grace"
then I guess you never went four wheeling
naked with your best friends in August
and ate hot dogs and drank champagne
and made up songs about each other
and traded sunglasses with each other
and graded the dawn with each other
and did coke off each others' eyelashes
without thinking of how to tell the story
later, because later is a crosseyed donkey.
Hang on. Is someone in trouble, boy? Shhh.
Say what? What do you mean we're fired?

Don't Pretend You Didn't Want To Go

O night of bacon and egg and cheese bagel
how serious it is to feel wonderful alone
and to know that I will probably die before
my friends, whom I judge for their pursuit of
exhibition and their always wanting to feel
things, to bruise apricots, that they are not in
parkas like those asleep in this Dunkin' Donuts
or imitating the sound of a motorcycle they
can't afford while they ride the last bus
over the river of indiscriminate light and I am
here to lick tinfoil and worry about my father,
who carries his love on the back of itself,
I am here to get Missed Connectioned by a fat
boy alone in his kitchen with his screen name,
here to fall asleep in a taxi and dream of the
same taxi but driven now by just a beard, who will
agree with everything I say, even when I say that
my topic is not direction for an audience of
clouds, that I wouldn't care if each of the clouds
just left, for they are not beautiful and neither are
pets, which I don't understand at all, as there are
names I've learned I will never need and don't carry
for oh it so wonderful to eat things that can't talk!
and for this I get up early and drive to breakfast
with you and also stay up very late and dumpster
dive at Whole Foods with you and drive to another
kind of breakfast at the diner where a man pointed
right here and said a thunder's gonna roll through those
boys then bang he made a finger gun -} I think he's
right because I don't care about Whole Foods or
jogging or the hammerhead shark or the ozone once
conceptualized to me as a bagel in trouble which is
silly I think in my night alone with this real bagel
but I do like redwoods, they're nice, and I do like

to like things, that is not the problem, like I like
skeet, coriander, espresso, chumscrubber, and
razzmatazz, which is mostly a kind of football play
that I want to run by leaving the field with the
ball, screaming MARS IS FOR EMOTIONAL and belly
flopping into a shallow kiddie pool wearing nothing
except TV antenna ears, sleep in a sleeping bag of
carrion guts and sing a karaoke of thunder hymnals
for we both know it's true that any language is just
an agreement to stop touching for a little while, which
allows me now to say that I shall miss my friends when I
die before them, which I will certainly do, death is the
best feeling, it puts all other feelings together without the
sheet, so bored and skeptical and bashfully consistent, it smells
like a boat shoe, it's better than being inside anything, even
death, better than all of the drugs in the world that learn
about you and shepherd you in zigzags through the great
big night, yet here I am already, and I wait to be known
before this, in the model of waiting for nothing that I cannot
know, by the tetherballs of searchlight that ignore me as I do.

for Alex & Jack

The Giant Who Learned to Dance

The truck is ready in the lawn
where we want this country to faint
tired as we are of espresso highs and spiders
the mountains high with sloe gin jars, and um but
you pricked the berries, so the jars are dry and full of
old nickels, golf tournaments and cysts, all of us—
meanwhile—occupied with lousy oars and reasons to
ford what we ford, left with this truck and a pair of
nylon baseball gloves, at attention left and right to
impress some dance upon it, moves we see in
others and chastise but practice in our razor mirrors,
tracing across our eyes (in Batusi V's) the route to
KFC and the cemetery, the graceless lack of distance
between all things, all fraught in the grass under the truck,
the night over the truck, and God if we could buy a day
off we would! Yet back he calls in bowls of yams, in a
deer at the back door, in the phone call from our
cousin about the Kevlar that saved his life, which is a
nice thing we guess, how we never saw Kevlar as
more than a word on television—until tonight—
how Kevlar sings, tonight, as an accordion peddler
in his too-tall hat, spit blitzing the glass of the truck
the bed of the truck the wheels of the truck down the
road of the truck, over the million ants: slaves for our
sedan chair (why do I feel gutless?) squeezing us through
and off the lot to the rigor and the salt, up to the hands we
reach with for soap, raise to fend, keep always ready to lock.

For You to Finish
While You're Swimming

Your heart is five eighths of a pound and fits inside of life
which will mostly be an evil pancake and a game of
tattoos you don't want, but sometimes good things
too: everybody on a bus laughing together at night,
towels just warm, dumping rock salt into homemade
ice cream, the scroll button on your mouse,
drinking coffee in the shower, then drinking coffee
together with your favorite naked person at the time
who will be a girl or a guy or a gluttony of sympathetic
polymers. Any one of these is fine. Ask your dad,
he's from California. Nik, be careful who you take a
nickname from. It's like they'll always have a hand
under your shirt. Names are secret fingers. Watch this:
yellowjacket, artichoke, huckleberry, marzipan.
Show up a minute late with a really awesome
story of what happened on the way. Listen in your
head before you say things out loud, try to know
reactions before people drop them but don't try
too hard, which is the same advice as, "Don't use
speakerphone, ever." When you take someone's
picture, show them. When you kiss someone's
neck, tell them a secret. If you do it right,
God will show up when you're mid-blink
like a fire that is also a window, like a trial by
snow, and you will want to close your eyes if
whispered to by one, and take your eyes and
heave them into the ocean for someone
else, which will feel both melodramatic and
perfect. Everything you feel will also be a way
to hold on. Social groups will always have that
one friend. There will be things you save to tell
someone that you'll never get to tell at all.

Fear is what happens when you sing too quietly.
One night you will go unexpectedly swimming,
then you won't need this poem anymore.
That's when to title me and dunk your mouth
and spit straight up so the water lands on your
face. Tell who you're with, "Look, a face!" and then
give your face to that person as hard as you can.

for Nikolai

Many thanks to the editors of the following publications, where some of these poems originally appeared: *No Tell Motel, Jellyfish, elimae, Sir!, Calaveras, Blu, Barnaby Jones, Robot Melon, Coconut, Lamination Colony, OCHO, Night Train, Concelebratory Shoehorn Review, Realpoetik, Brave Men Coinsides, isReads, Notnostrums, Everyday Genius, Glitterpony, La Fovea, Invisible Ear,* and *LIT*.

Deep thanks: my family & my friends
& the strangers of notable grace.

Mike Young is also the author of *Look! Look! Feathers* (Word Riot Press 2010). He co-edits *NOÖ Journal* and *Magic Helicopter Press*. He lives in Northampton, MA, and he can be found online at mikeayoung.blogspot.com.